Christmas Ornaments
A Festive Study

by Margaret Schiffer

Schiffer Publishing Ltd

Santa Claus standing beside a chimney is an iron bank
made by J. and E. Stevens. It was patented October 15,
1889, and measures 6" x 4".

DEDICATION

Dedicated to my grandchildren Bert, Peter and Edward, the
future collectors.

Copyright 1984 © by Margaret B. Schiffer.
Edited by Judith E. Riddell.
Library of Congress Catalog Number: 84-50805.

Printed in the United States of America.
ISBN: 0-88740-011-6
Published by Schiffer Publishing Limited, Box E, Exton, Pennsylvania
19341.
This book may be purchased from the publisher. Please include $1.50
postage.
Try your bookstore first.

Thoughts About Christmas

For most of us, Christmas brings fond memories of childhood; of clustering around the Christmas tree with our families in the wee hours of the morning after spending weeks in fast-pulsed anticipation. The long-awaited day inevitably would begin with a moment of speechless, tingling excitement, as the culmination of weeks of preparation was viewed in its entirety.

One of the happiest of these preparations was certainly the decorating. Bringing the ornaments which had been so carefully packed away the year before down from the attic heightened holiday pleasure. Each family member would want to hang his favorite ornament in the most prominent position on the tree. The placement of each decoration would be the subject of delicious debate: should the tiny Steinway be hung next to the bright orange zepplin, or beside Mary Pickford? Should Jolly Saint Nick be framed with candy canes or gingerbread men? "Silent Night" would be interrupted by a boisterous free for all with tinsel nearly every year. Ultimately, the tree trimmers would wear more of it than the tree.

Although it has been years since some of us were children, trimming the tree with the old ornaments can still reawaken the wonder of Christmas within us as we hang familiar favorites on fragrant green boughs. Delicate bells and molded glass horns start the joyous music of Christmas ringing in our ears; gilded stars remind us of the glorious light that shone from the star of Bethlehem; jolly Santas and miniature toys bring back mornings of bright-eyed expectation. We remember the sumptuous aromas coming from Mother's kitchen, the scrumptious treats which were served once a year, the resonant timbre of Father's voice as he read the Christmas stories aloud, and the family unity which seemed even stronger during that enchanted season of sharing.

In the following pages, we will relive the wonders of Christmases past. Through pictures of the ornaments that enthalled us as children, we will pay tribute to the magic of Christmas, which brings out the best in all of us.

The tin clockwork Santa Claus driving a sleigh drawn by goats was made in the late 1800s, and is attributed to Althof Bergmann. Santa has a composition face, wooden body, and is dressed in crepe paper.

This majestic papier mache Santa Claus manufactured at the turn of the century is similar to one used on a G.A. Schwartz (Philadelphia PA) trading card. He is 26" tall. These Santas are known to have been made in smaller sizes.

The German Santa Claus in the unusual hat adorned with a pine cone and yellow nesting bird is 12" tall. He was made of papier mache at the turn of the century.

Knect Ruppert is the servant of the Christ Child. On December 6 he collects the lists of children to whom the Christ Child later brings gifts. This candy box was made in England at the turn of the century, and stands 11" tall.

Belsnickles carrying switches originated in Germany. This one is 12" tall and was produced at the turn of the century.

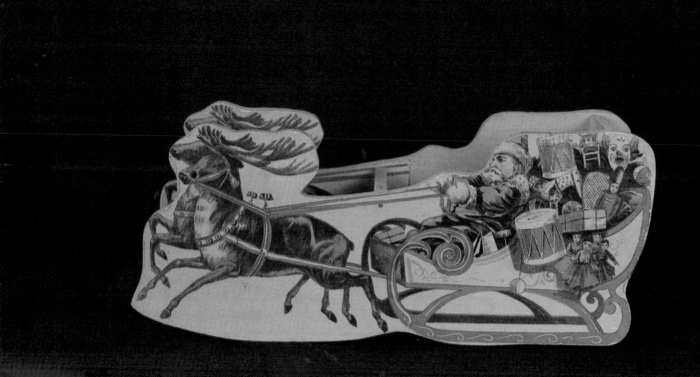

'Walking Man'' Santa Claus was patented September 21, 1875 by Jues Blakeslee & Williams Co. of Bridgeport CT. The body is wood covered by fabric; the head and hands are slush casting.

Lithographed paper on this wooden Santa Claus and sleigh is attributed to Bliss. Made in the late 1800s, it is 12 1/4'' long.

Composition Santa Claus candy container was made in Germany at the turn of the century. Trimmed with mica, imitation fur, and Dresden stars, it is 15 1/2'' high.

Gnome-like papier mache Santa Claus candy container was made at the turn of the century in Germany. The unusually tall figure (31 1/2'') is cloth-coated, and separates at the waist to reveal a box which could be filled with sweets.

Iron Santa Claus and sleigh attributed to Hubley of Lancaster, PA. The sleigh is 15'' long, and was made in the early 20th century.

Iron Santa Claus and sleigh attributed to Kyser and Rex. The toy measures 17'' long from the back of the sleigh to the tip of Prancer's front hoof.

German papier mache Santa Claus was made at the turn of the century.

The German Belsnickles lining the bottom of the page range from 5'' to 6''. Made before 1917, the smaller ones were less detailled and may not have been hand-painted.

Papier mache Belsnickles are totally hollow, having been cast in a mold in two sections (back and front). Made in Germany from the 1870s to 1917, the figures range in size from 14" to 7 3/4". The most common colors found are white, yellow, red, and blue; the rarest include green, brown, purple, pink, and black. The bottoms of the figures may be covered or left open.

The papier mache Belsnickles shown here were made in Germany prior to 1917. Ranging in size from 10 1/4'' to 8'', all but one carry feather trees. The Santa with the open red coat and blue trousers is not a common example.

Late nineteenth century Santa Claus plaque made in Germany is 6 1/2'' x 5 1/2''.

Pull toys have long been a favorite of young children. This papier mache Santa Claus and reindeer pull toy must have been no exception. The toy was made before 1917. The sleigh, which is made of wood as is the 16 3/4" platform, is filled with penny toys and Dresden ornaments.

Papier mache (left), cardboard (center), and crepe paper attired (right) Santa Clauses were made in Germany in the early 20th century. The third and sixth Santas from the left are candy containers. The fourth Santa from the left is marked "Germany" on the enclosed bottom. The thin back piece is often stapled to the front of the cardboard figures.

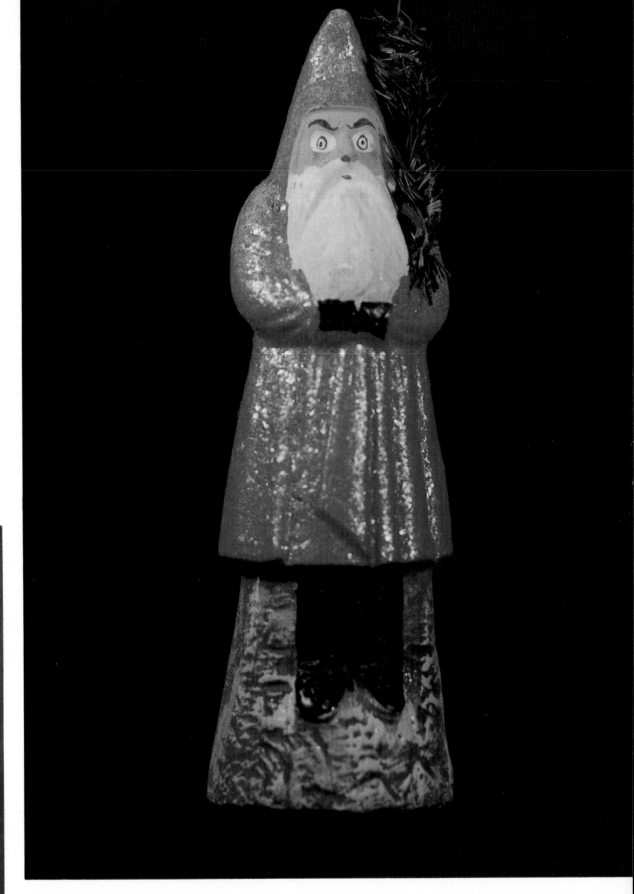

Papier mache Belsnickle with an unusual shape is marked "Germany", and stands 10 1/4" high. The Belsnickle, an elvish old man with a long white beard, was St. Nicholas's companion on Christmas Eve. The plump, merry imp brought sugarplums to good children, and switches to the bad ones.

A set of Santa Claus Snow Babies, still in the original box, was made by Karl Schneider in Germany during the early 20th century. Close scrutiny reveals the careful attention to detail on these tiny figures.

Nine inch papier mache Belsnickle made in Germany before 1917. He carries a pressed paper tree, and sports fabric trim around his hood.

Papier mache Santa Claus made in Germany in the early 20th century. His coat is made of cloth. He carries a brass basket on his back, and the candle in his lantern lights up. He is 9 1/2" tall.

No one is more universally loved than Santa Claus. He has been immortalized in song and story, celebrated in ritual and verse, and of course commemorated in Christmas ornaments. This jolly symbol of Christmas is based on St. Nicholas, Bishop of Myra, who lived during the fourth century. St. Nicholas was so benevolent that he became a legend in his own lifetime, and even after he died, his spirit lived on. Good St. Nick as we know him is a gift of the heart. He is a composite of all that is kind and generous in men: he is the spirit of selfless giving, of sharing and of love. Santa's name, clothes and even his appearance vary from country to country or one century to another, but these superficial differences cannot disguise the spirit of love that is Santa Claus. We never become so old that Saint Nick is not alive in our hearts; the spirit of giving and of Christmas never dies. It is not surprising that Kris Kringle appears more frequently than any other figure during the Christmas season; and that the most beloved of all Christmas ornaments depict him. Like Christmas itself, he is an inspiration to all of us.

These are all papier mache Santa Clauses except the second from the right, which has a bisque head and wooden arms. All are German cloth-coated candy containers, and range in size from 7'' to 12''.

At the turn of a key, this turn of the century German composition Santa Claus nods. He is 34'' tall, cloth-coated and his basket holds 20th century toys.

PAPIER MACHE CANDY CONTAINERS

Christmas would not be complete without candy. A wide variety of dynamic, boldly-hued candy containers was produced during the 19th century to amaze and delight children. Jolly Santas and leering devils, prancing reindeer and bulging stockings held sugary surprises for deserving youngsters. These candy holders were generally made of papier mache, but tulle candy bags with celluloid faces were not unusual. Often, small wicker baskets were filled with sweets and hung on the tree. Although many Christmas decorations are more beautiful, not one of them is as popular with children as the most humble candy container.

Papier mache Santa Claus candy container produced in Germany at the turn of the century. His brown cloth coat is rare (most are red). Santa is 20 1/2" tall.

Papier mache Santa Claus candy container bearing a festive feather tree is 21" tall. Santa was made in Germany at the turn of the century. He wears a snow-covered cloth coat cinched with a rope belt. His beard is rabbit fur.

Bisque Santa Clauses were made in Germany at the beginning of the 20th century. The taller 8" Santa and the 7" Santa seated on a cardboard candy container log have bisque heads and hands. Their clothing is crepe paper trimmed with cotton batting on the hat and cuffs.

Cotton Santa Claus handkerchief made by the Oriental Print Works. The picture was derived from a picture by Thomas Nast.

In its original uncut state, this cotton Santa Claus doll, which bears a striking resemblance to the cotton Santa Claus handkerchief shown above, was obviously influenced by a Thomas Nast picture. This doll was probably made by E.S. Peck of Brooklyn, NY, who patented the pattern December 20, 1886.

Kris Kringle Picture Cubes (Blocks) were copyrighted in 1896 by McLaughlin Bros., NY. The blocks can be put together to make pictures.

Around the World With Santa Claus is a cube puzzle that can be put together in a variety of ways to show numerous scenes from Santa Claus' travels. McLaughlin Bros. of New York copyrighted this puzzle in 1889.

With the exception of the woman, all figures in this clockwork animated picture c. 1880s and 1890s move. Little Brother plays his drum, Sister rocks her doll, Big Brother rides his hobby horse, Grandpa bounces Baby on his knee, and Santa views the Christmas merriment from the window.

Lithographed paper on cardboard Santa Claus delivers a doll to a sleeping child too excited to go to bed. This 34 1/2" figure was made in Germany from 1880 to the 1890s.

Sprightly Santa Claus jumps out of the box when the latch is released. This German jack-in-the-box was made between 1880 and the 1890s.

Fairy Land Rail Road blocks were made in America at the turn of the century.

Painted wooden Santa Claus doll made in the late 19th century, possibly in Pennsylvania. Pull the ring under his skirt and the doll flaps its arms as its mask flips back, showing a man's face.

Possibly made in France, this cotton batting Santa Claus has a papier mache face. He was made in the 1890s to hang from a string attached to his neck. He is 13 1/2'' tall, with a label that mentions the Wanamaker stores and the price of $1.00.

Spagnam moss Santa Claus, made in Germany at the turn of the century. Santa has a papier mache face with a cotton beard, and is 8 1/2'' high.

This early 20th century German Santa Claus rides a nodding donkey. Santa has a papier mache face, hands, and boots, a rabbit fur beard, and a cloth coat and hat trimmed with lichen. The donkey is cloth-covered wood.

Papier mache Santa Claus and his candy container reindeer made in Germany in the early 20th century. Santa wears a cloth coat and has a rabbit fur beard. His 14" sleigh is wooden, and is laden with delightful 20th century toys.

Papier mache Santa Claus is made up of five pieces: the head, the beard, the body and the two legs. The 27" figure was used for advertising, and according to the label affixed to the base, was made in 1906 by the National Papier Mache Works of Ohio.

Early 20th century German Santa Claus riding a skin-covered wood donkey. Santa has papier mache face, hands, and boots, a cloth coat and hat, and a rabbit fur beard.

←

Copyright 1906 by W. E. Richardson.

MANUFACTURED BY NATIONAL PAPIER MACHE WORKS

Santa Claus riding a reindeer is a German candy container made around the turn of the century. Santa has a papier mache face, hands, and boots, a rabbit fur beard, and wears a cloth coat. The reindeer is cloth-covered wood.

Roly poly papier mache Santa Clauses made by Schoenhut of Philadelphia in the early 20th century range from 11 1/2" to 6 1/4".

Chalk Santa Clauses were probably made in Pennsylvania around the turn of the century. The blue Santa is 22''; the gold Santa is 8''. The original tree is attached with wire.

Paper Santa Claus and his sleigh is attributed to Raphael Tuck of London and was printed between 1871, when the first Christmas greetings were published, and the 1890s.

Papier mache Santa Claus lanterns were made in Germany during the early 20th century. They measure from 5 1/2" high by 8" wide to 3" x 5 1/4".

Santa Claus is getting an early start on his Christmas deliveries this year. Filled to overflowing with 20th century toys, his 16 1/2" wire and crepe paper sleigh is ready for another night of spreading Christmas cheer. The ribbons and bells adorning the sleigh are original. Santa boasts a crisp red cloth coat for the occasion, and his rabbit fur beard is "as white as the snow". His reindeer are papier mache candy containers. Santa and his sleigh were made in Germany before 1914.

"You'd better be good for goodness' sake" admonishes this stern composition Santa. Made in Germany in the early 20th century, Santa's clothing is brown fabric, and he carries a general and European heads over his shoulder.

Kindly composition Santa nods, as does his cloth covered reindeer. Santa, who measures 26 1/2" from his head to his foot, has glass eyes and a cloth coat and hat.

Santas on wood sleighs.

Japanese Santa Clauses on sleds, c. 1925. All Santas have composition faces, rabbit fur beards and cloth bodies.

41

Composition Saint Nicholas bearing the three gifts is a candy container made in Austria. Made in the early 20th century, Saint Nicholas is 10 3/4'' tall. The good Saint's splendid garments are cloth, and he has a label which reads ''A gerstner zuckerbacker confectioneer Wien — Vienna, Austria. Karnthner Strasse 6 Carinthia''.

Cotton batting Santa Claus made in the early 20th century. He has a composition face, and stands a full 18'' high. On the underside of the base is part of a label with Cyrillic lettering, which would seem to indicate that this Santa originated in Russia.   →

Santa Claus delivers Christmas trees from this wooden sleigh pulled by metal reindeer. Made in Germany around the turn of the century, the sleigh measures 15" in length. The trees are German as well.

German Santa Claus in his sleigh full of 20th century toys. The composition reindeer and wooden sleigh is 32 1/2" long, and may be German. ↓

The short jackets, belts, and blue trousers worn by these papier mache Santa Claus candy containers are typical of 20th century Santas. The German Santas measure 15" and 11", and their beards are made of rabbit fur.

German composition Santa Clauses were made in the 20th century. The Santa on the left is 7" tall; his thoughtful companion is 6" tall.   →

The Santa Claus depicted here adorns the cover of a 20th century paintbox.   →

Any man can become Santa Claus for a day while wearing this papier mache Santa Claus mask, which was made in Germany at the turn of the century.

Cloth-covered Santa Clauses made in Germany and Japan in the 20th century. Their faces, hands, and boots are composition.

Twentieth century Santa Claus plate was a premium given away by the C.D. Kenny Company, who sold coffee and spices.

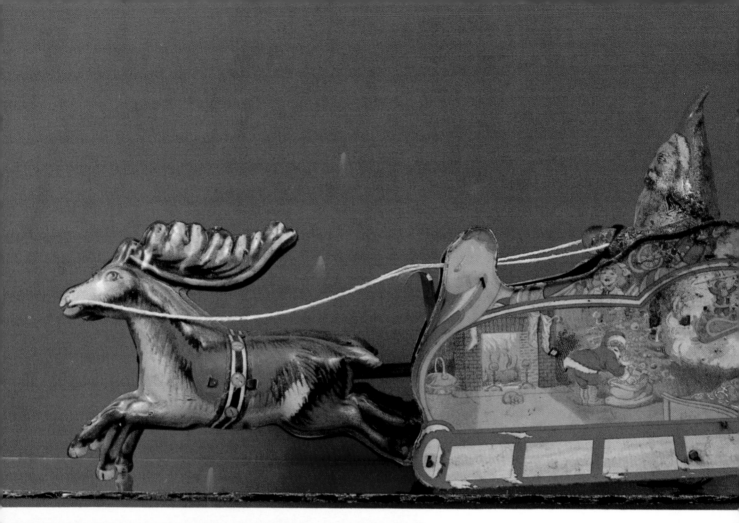

"Santee Claus", one of the "Strauss Mechanical Toys" made by the Ferdinand Strauss Corporation of New York, was patented October 18, 1921. The toy is painted tin, and measures 11" long.

Composition Santa Clauses made in Japan in the mid 20th century. They range from 7" to 9 1/2" high, and their clothing is made of cloth or paper. →

Composition Santa Claus poses next to an apt likeness of himself on a paper bell. Seated Santa and the Santa bell were made in Japan during the 20th century.

This impressed cardboard store sign was made during the twentieth century, and stands a remarkable 35'' high.

Santa Claus's image appears on a variety of household objects, including this 8" brass bank and 3" Japanese pot metal cigarette lighter.

Santa Claus is also a favorite subject for cake and chocolate molds made of iron and tin. Made during the early 20th century, these Santas came in a variety of sizes and interpretations. The larger Santa Claus is a foot tall. Three smaller variations measure 1/4".

← Painted cardboard Santa Clauses were made in the 20th century. The plump Santa getting ready to descend the chimney (left) is 8 3/4" tall, and the Santa on the right is 9 1/2" tall. His label reads "Made in England, Patented".

Paper stand up Santa Clauses and trees were made from the 1930s onward. The large Santa on the left is 10" tall, the tree is 11 1/2", and the small Santa is 9".

Paper tower Santa Clauses and Santa bells ← made in Japan from 1930s onward. ↓

Glass Santa Claus candy containers. The Santa on the left was made by the Victory Glass Company.

Celluloid Santa Clauses and sleighs were made in the mid 20th century, probably in Japan.

Paper and fabric candy containers in the shape of boots were made in the 20th century, and hung on the tree.

Tin Santa Claus marked "J. Chein Co. Made in U.S.A." is 5 1/2" tall.

Santa Claus pushing a wheel barrow.

The painted cast iron bank on the left was an advertising promotion made in the 1930s. The Santa Claus with the spring neck is also a bank, and was probably made in Japan. ↓

Pressed paper 16" Santa and 19 1/4" tree were made after 1930.

Printed paper "scrap" Santa is part of a scrapbook dated 1884. Santa carries a Christmas tree, toys and sugarplums for good children, and a bundle of switches for bad ones.

Detailled 18 1/4" chalk church hides a candle inside its elegant facade. When the candle is lit, celestial light streams from the glass windows.

Twelve inch tin church also holds a candle. Though the church is simple in design, it is breathtaking when lit up.

58

In the 1880s scrapbooks made from printed paper "scraps" were quite popular. This is a page from a scrapbook dated 1884. The paper cutout depicts an early Victorian tabletop tree, decorated with sugarplums, kugel, and flickering white tapers.

HOMEMADE

The earliest and perhaps most innovative Christmas ornaments were homemade. Commercially manufactured ornaments were not available until 1870, so each family had to harness the artistic abilities of its members in order to decorate the home. Natural objects were frequently used: fresh greenery, pine cones, nuts, fruits, and flowers. The ladies of the house also spent the weeks before Christmas baking fragrant, delectable sweetmeats for their families to hang on the Christmas tree. Victorian families often made gaily decorated paper cornucopias and gilded eggshells which had been carefully halved and saved for weeks beforehand to hold these delightful confections. Brightly colored chromolithographs trimmed with scraps of tinsel or angel hair were interspersed with strings of popcorn and cranberries to achieve a festive, homespun look. These appealing decorations are cherished for the warm, homey aspect they give a Christmas tree, and for their uniquely personal creativity.

Homemade cardboard flat ornaments characterized early Victorian Christmas trees. These decorations strive for simple elegance with lace and gold paper trim.

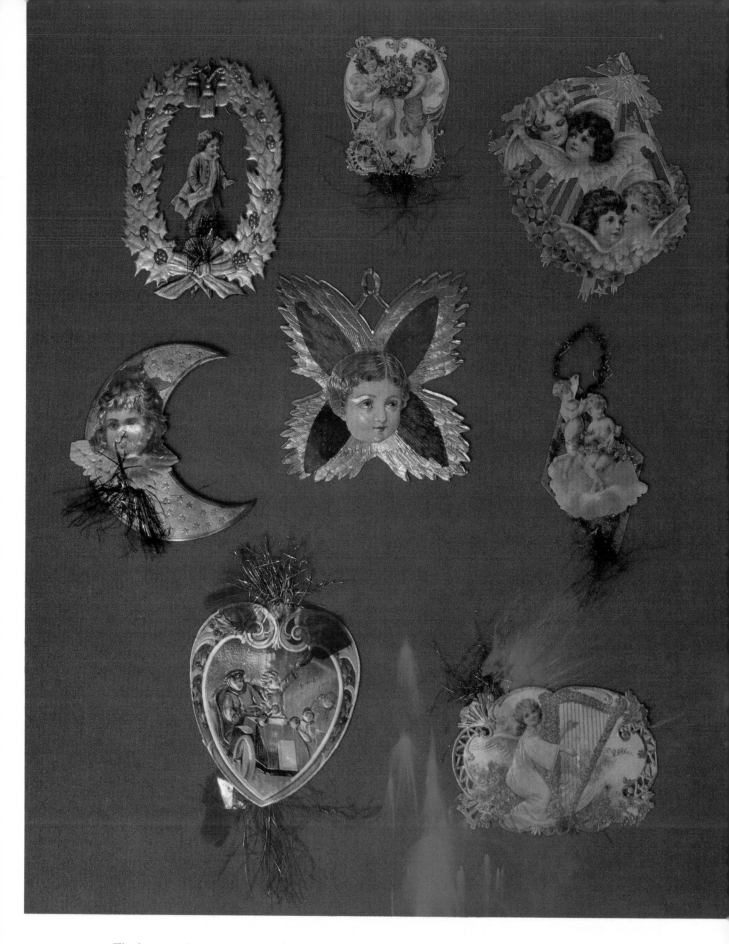

The homemade ornaments on these two pages are made from embossed color prints embellished with tinsel rope.

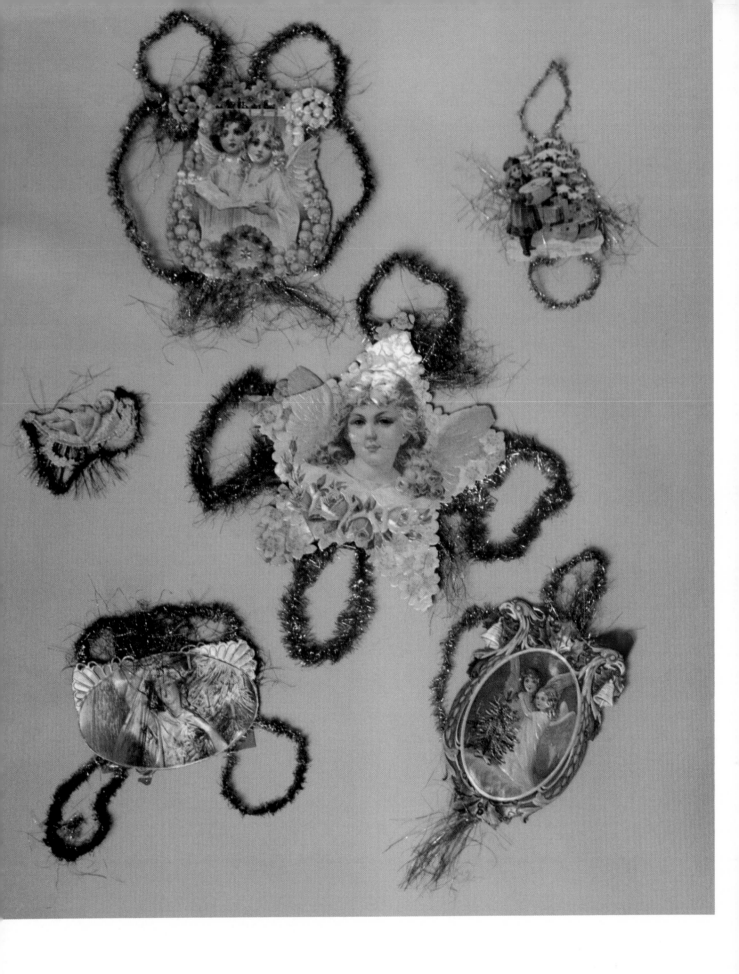

Made from color prints, cotton batting, tinsel rope, and Dresden stars, these handmade ornaments impart a distinctive Victorian flavor.

64

The handcrafted ornaments on these two pages show how simple materials like tinsel rope, gold paper, Dresden stars, paper lace, color prints, and thin transparent muslin can be combined to make ornaments that add sparkling grandeur to any Christmas tree.

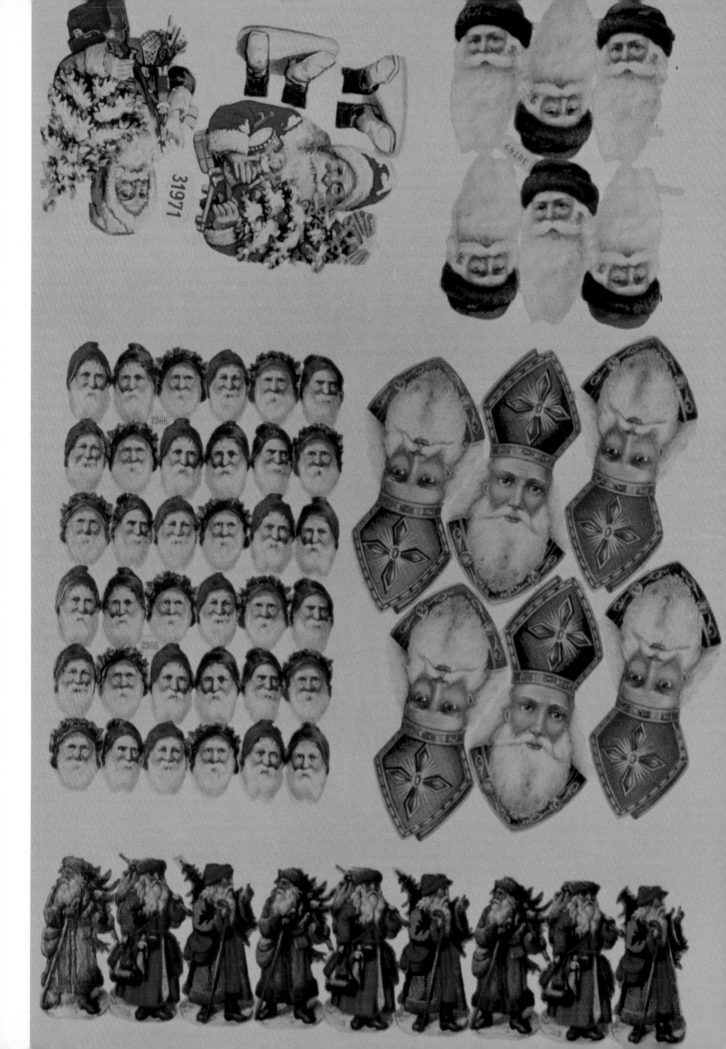

A sheet of printed paper scraps manufactured to be cut up and assembled, characteristic of the sheets firms began mass producing around 1875.

Spun glass endows the chromolithographic prints on these homemade ornaments with ethereal beauty.

omemade ornaments made from printed paper scraps, tinsel rope, spun ass, cotton batting, and crepe paper have a distinct bucolic charm.

Metal ornaments.

TIN

in ornaments were the first non-edible Christmas ornaments to be made ommercially available. Between 1870 and 1900, tin decorations in many apes were popular in America. They were so lightweight that the slightest raught of air would cause them to sway into slow, graceful motion. Tin irds, fish, and animals thrill children because they appear to fly, swim or rance. Decorated with tiny mirrorlike facets and colorful glass jewels, they nd a majestic aspect to the humblest of homes.

anta Claus made from printed paper scraps, cotton batting, and crepe aper.   →

Metal and Czechoslovakian glass bead ornaments.

Metal ornaments, a few of which are trimmed with tinsel rope.

This antique feather tree is trimmed with Dresden, cotton, glass, wood, composition, metal, and paper ornaments. At the base are Dresden ornaments and part of a painted tin village.

A menagerie of Dresden ornaments inhabit this page and the pages that follow. The rabbit with the glass eyes is marked "Germany".

DRESDENS

Of all Christmas ornaments ever manufactured, Dresdens are among the most exquisite. Most of these extraordinarily detailed decorations were meticulously handcrafted in Germany between 1880 and 1910 in a limitless assortment of fascinating shapes. By candlelight, Dresdens appear to be made of carefully etched gold or silver. But surprisingly, these charming masterpieces in miniature are fashioned from embossed cardboard. Nevertheless, their regal beauty is unrivaled by even the most elaborate ornaments; and they add subtle elegance to even the simplest tree.

Dresden birds.

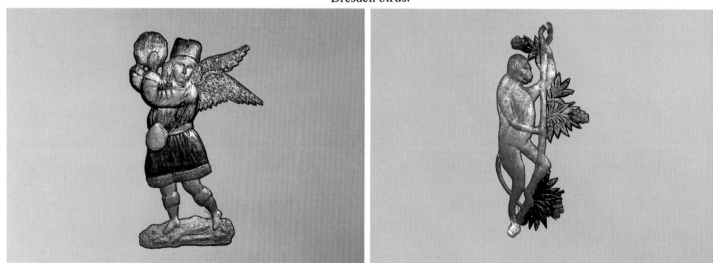

The silk bags attached to the animal masks were filled with candy.

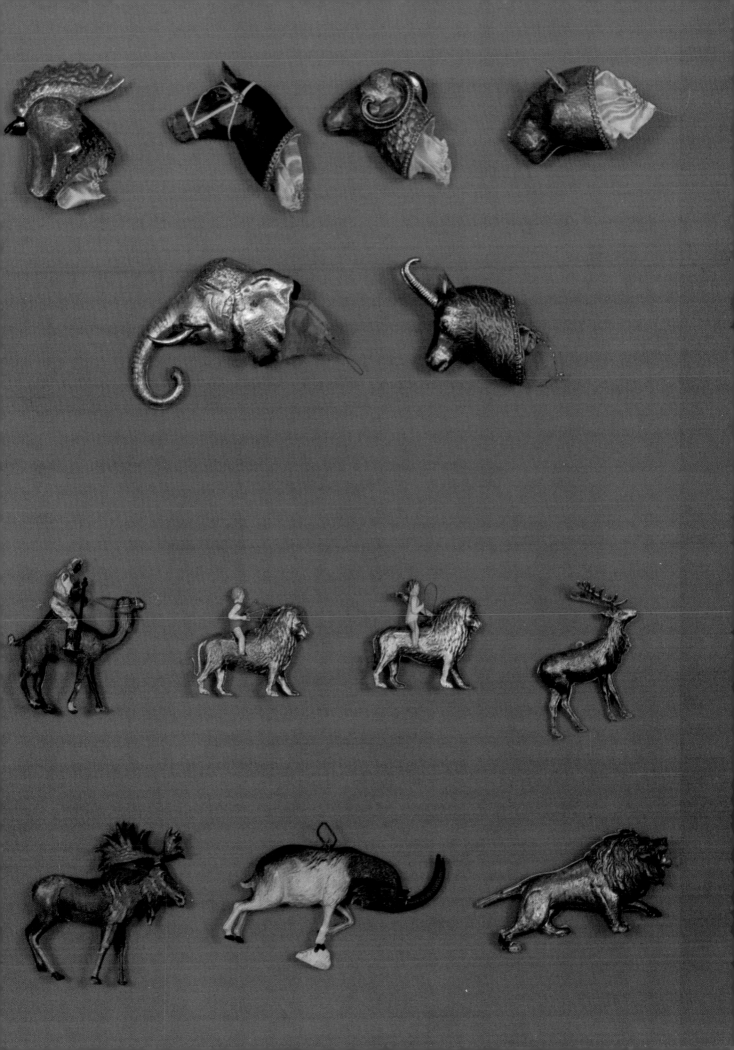

Many German companies specialized in Dresden ornaments between 1880 and 1910. They were more popular in Germany than they were in America, however, because Americans preferred the less expensive glass ornaments.

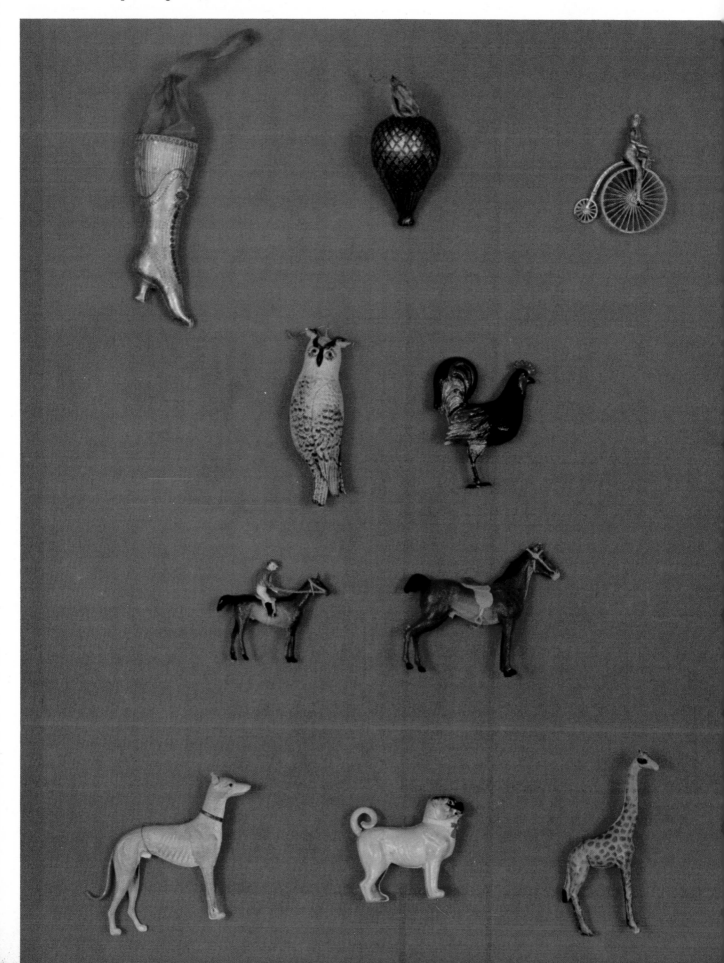

Musical instruments, fashion accessories and everyday household items were replicated in miniature by the skilled German artisans who made these Dresden ornaments. The silver boot in the picture on the right is marked "FURTH".

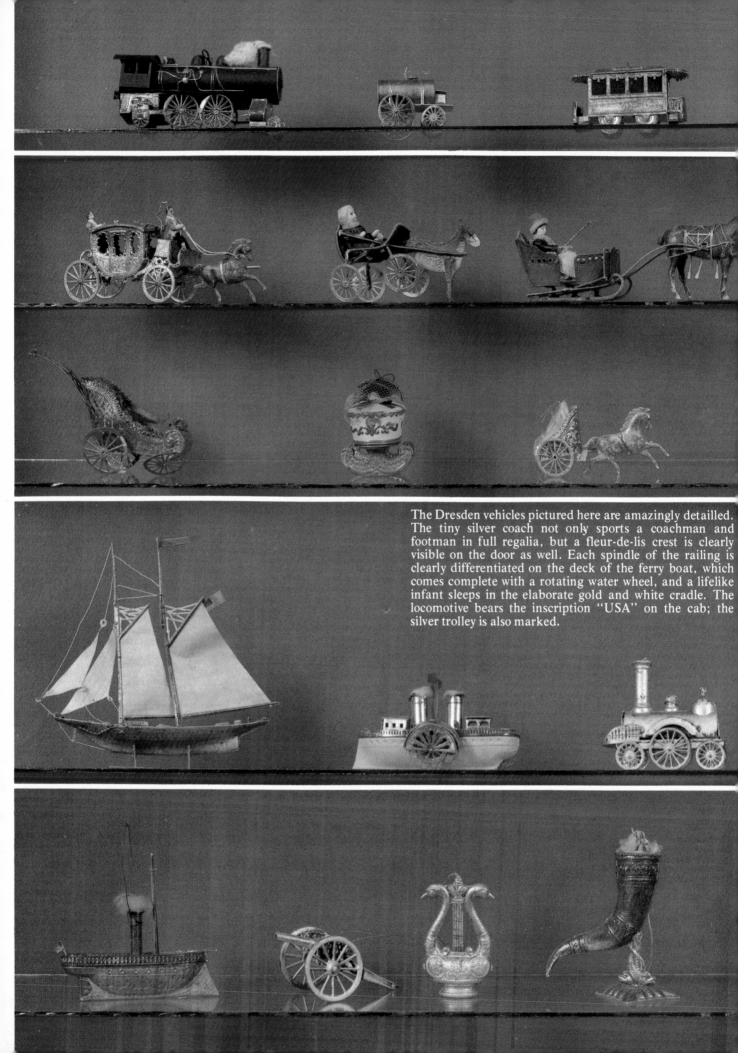

The Dresden vehicles pictured here are amazingly detailled. The tiny silver coach not only sports a coachman and footman in full regalia, but a fleur-de-lis crest is clearly visible on the door as well. Each spindle of the railing is clearly differentiated on the deck of the ferry boat, which comes complete with a rotating water wheel, and a lifelike infant sleeps in the elaborate gold and white cradle. The locomotive bears the inscription "USA" on the cab; the silver trolley is also marked.

Although these Dresdens are small scale copies of articles which were fairly common in Victorian households, the ornaments themselves are so rare today that most people have never seen one.

Ordinary objects were made decorative through the artistry of Dresden ornament makers.

Dresden globe candy containers allowed Victorian parents to give their children the world at Christmastime.

Colored Dresden Santa Clauses are unusual. Most flat Dresden ornaments are gold or silver like those on the facing page.

Vivid color gives these Dresdens their splendour. Like all flat Dresdens, they are decorated on one side only.

Dresden barnyard animals and a rare Santa Claus in his sleigh.

(Top) Dresden flat ornaments. (Bottom) Paper candy containers. The one on the right is marked "Merry Christmas, Happy New Year. Copyright 1877 by Cornwell & Skelton, Birmingham Conn."

Paper, cloth and straw cornucopias were used to hold candy, popcorn, and nuts.

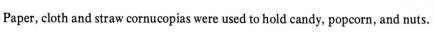

MOLDED

Molded ornaments, which were perfected in 1890, have a wider selection of shapes than any other. These glass decorations came in a variety of colors and sizes, and depicted designs from nature; whimsical animals; musical instruments; vehicles; geometric figures; buildings; and a variety of religious and fictional characters; including Betty Boop, Punch and Judy, and the Man in the Moon. Some of these ornaments are rich in detail, some twinkle with diamond dust, and others glisten with minute glass beads.

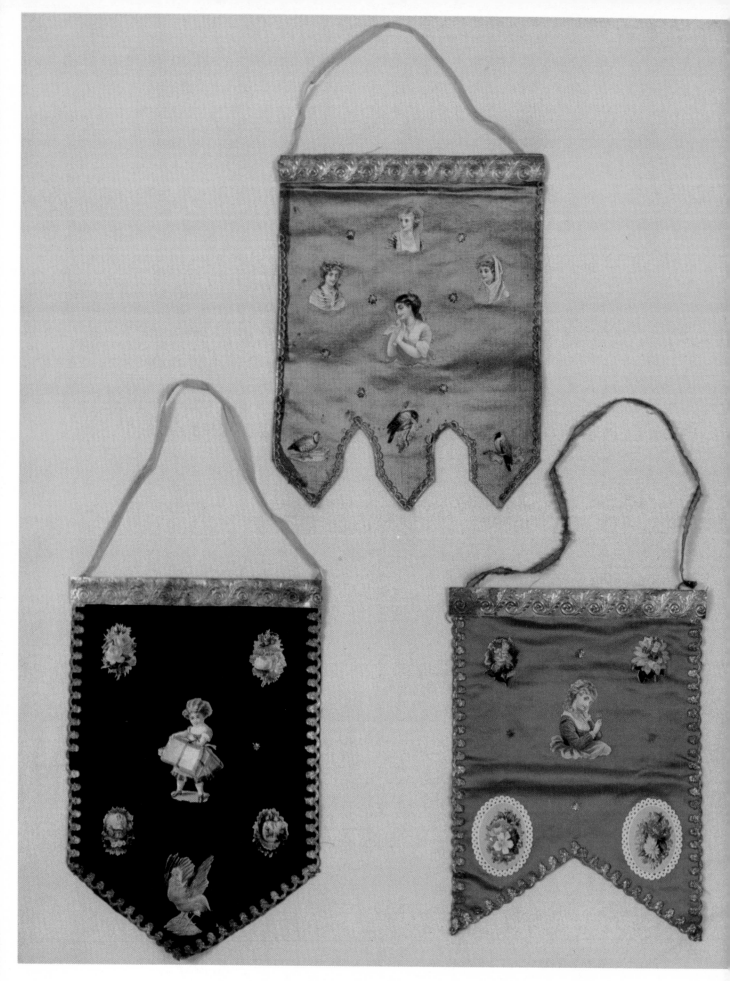

Silk banners were decorated with paper scraps, paper lace, and Dresden stars.

Woven baskets shown with glass fruit ornaments, and paper baskets that could be filled with candy.

Many of these glass bird ornaments have spun glass tails.

Colorful painted cotton birds hung on many Victorian Christmas trees. The spring clip, which was replaced by round loop hangers, was used to clamp antique ornaments to the Christmas tree.

Composition birds on swings.

Assorted glass birds show the Victorian iiking for plumes, spun glass feathers, and ropes of tinsel.

Exquisite blue glass animals and birds show a rare purity of form and fluidity of line. ↓

Songbirds in glass and metal cages were popular, as were glass deer.

Jolly glass clowns in colorful costumes

108

Several of these glass fish have spun glass tails.

A holiday garden of glass flowers. Those that clip onto the tree are often older than those with a metal loop hanger.

Glass vegetables in imaginative colors, and glass and gilded paper nuts.

Sparkling cotton fruit and vegetables. Some of the fruits and other miscellaneous forms have tinsel decoration.

me glass fruits have leaves attached, others are decorated with fine strands of tinsel rope.

xquisite glass teapots.

ousehold items were popular, as were glass floral ornaments.

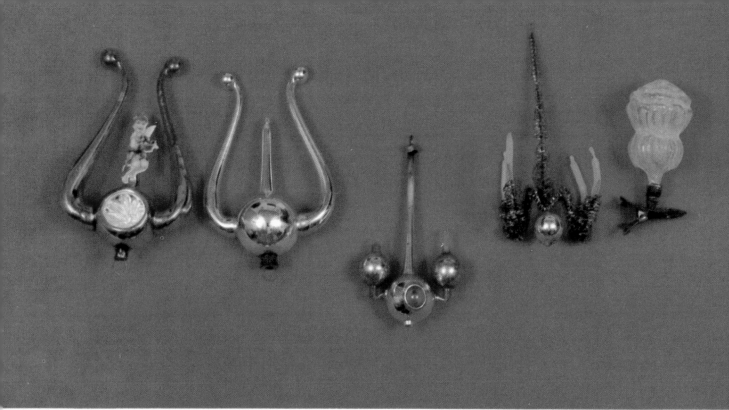

Glass pipes

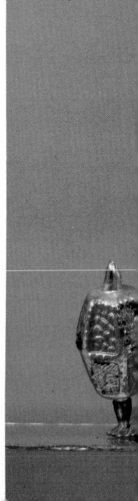

Glass lamps, chandeliers, and other lighting fixtures.

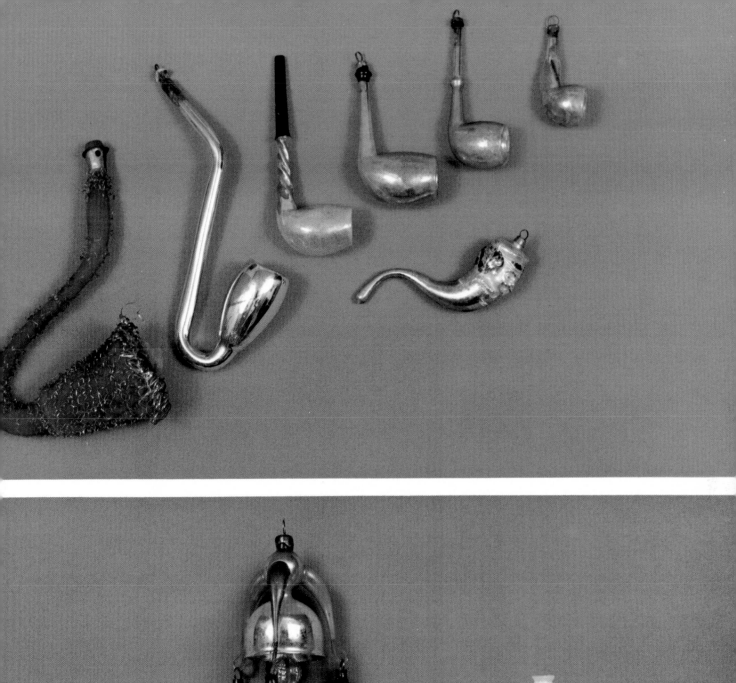

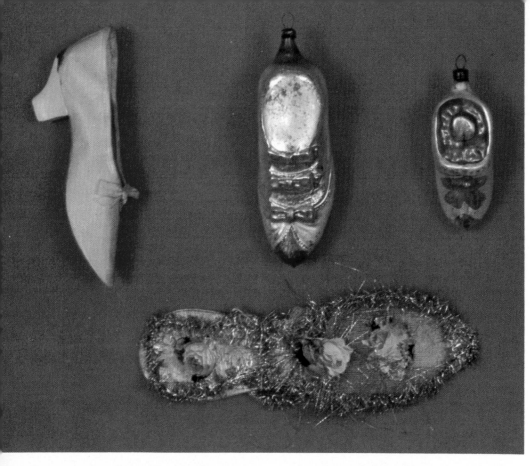

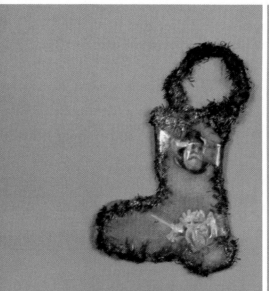

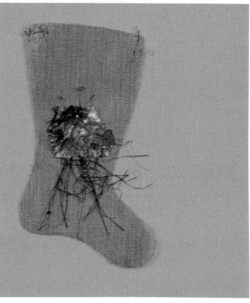

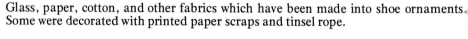

Glass, paper, cotton, and other fabrics which have been made into shoe ornaments. Some were decorated with printed paper scraps and tinsel rope.

KUGEL

Glassblowers in Lauscha, Germany have fashioned Kugels since 1820. By 1840, what had started as a way of passing the time turned into a successful industry. The sturdy, colorful ornaments which resulted from the glassblowers' game were not sold in America until 1880, however, when a young merchant named Woolworth bought $25 worth on the condition that he would be able to return them if he couldn't sell them. Two days later, Woolworth had sold the last of them; and by 1890 he ordered 200,000 kugels a year. Although they were not the earliest decorations ever made, these shimmering orbs are considered the most traditional ornaments by many. They were the forerunner of modern day Christmas balls, which are still the most popular Christmas ornaments. Yet today's mass-produced Christmas balls lack the character of the kugel ornaments produced in 19th century Germany, whose lustrous beauty recaptures the essence of an old-fashioned Christmas.

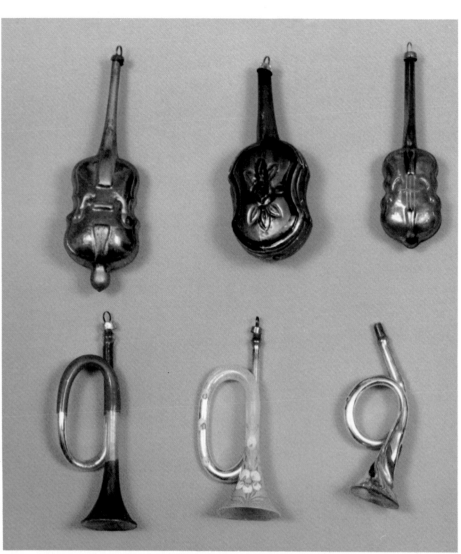

Blown glass musical instruments.
← Kugel ornaments in a variety of forms.
↓

Wax and papier mache angels with a paper sunburst.

Paper and cloth flag ornaments.

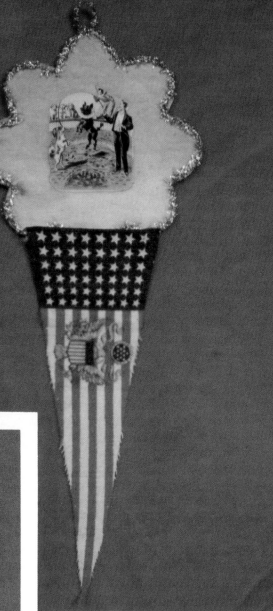

Patriotic ornaments made of paper,
cotton batting, papier mache, and tinsel r

Glass figural ornaments depicted a large
variety of subjects from cartoon characters
to historical noteworthies; and from stage
personalities to American Indians.

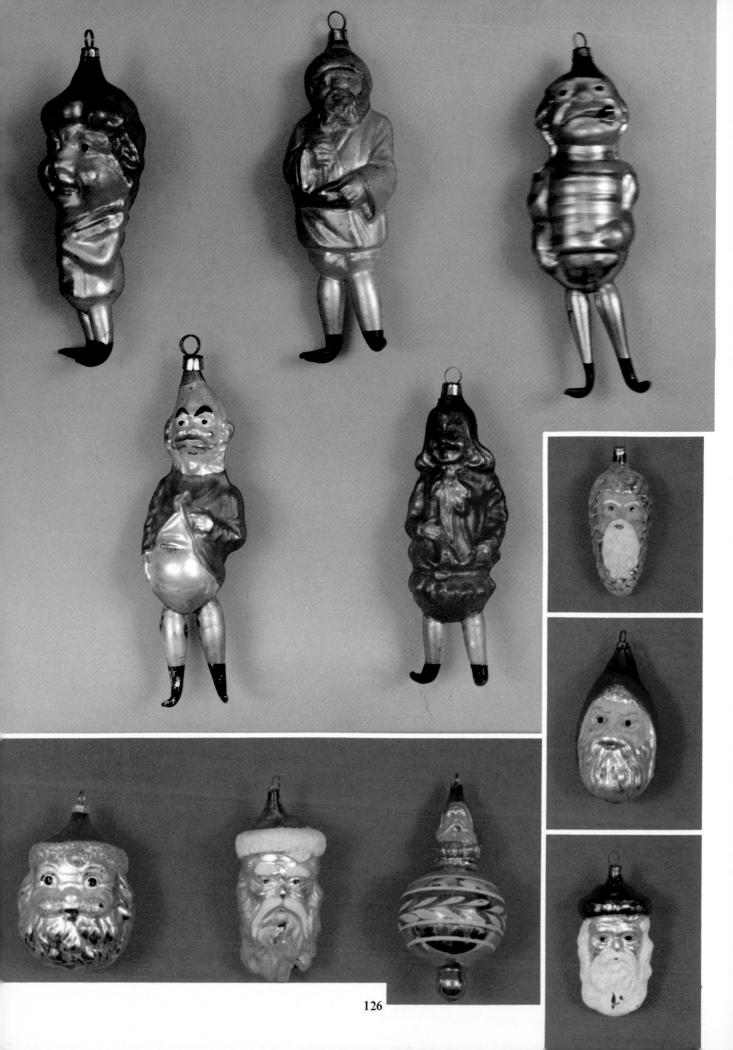

Glass people and Santa heads showing imaginative design and colorful painting.

Candy or nut containers with celluloid heads, and net bodies. Some have cloth trousers.

Cotton Santa Claus ornaments with printed paper faces. Glass balls and tinsel rope have been used for decoration.

Papier mache Santa Claus ornaments ranging in size from 2 1/2" to 3".

Fine craftsmanship may be seen in the intricate molding and detailled painting on these glass Santa Clauses.

← Glass Santa Clauses, each with a distinct personality.

Santa Claus squeak toy ornament has a papier mache face, wooden hands and feet, and a cardboard stomach. Pull a → string in his hat and he squeaks.

Cotton Santa Claus ornaments.

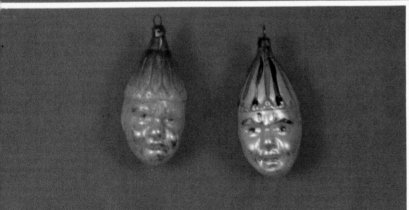

WAX

Wax, with its nearly lifelike appearance under candlelight, was an inevitable medium for Christmas figures. Children, animals, and even the Christ child were molded in wax, looking for all the world as though they might speak at any moment. The most convincing of these wax ornaments are angels like the one shown on page 122. Wings outstretched, these celestial figures hover serenely over the tree branches, calling to mind the true meaning of Christmas.

Woman with wax face and paper clothing.

Glass faces.

133

Glass people and snowmen.   Jointed composition people with detailled painting and molding.

Cotton girls with painted paper faces are decorated with
crepe paper, tinsel rope, and Dresden stars.

...tton people dressed with cotton batting or crepe paper, ...me trimmed with Dresden stars. The faces were ...equently painted directly on the cotton.

COTTON

...ft cotton ornaments have been among those most beloved ...y children. Because they were inexpensive and unbreak-...ble, even the smallest child could help decorate the Christ-...as tree. These ornaments could be clothed in crepe paper ...d sprinkled with glass shavings, which glistened like ...ew-fallen snow. Sparkling beneath the Christmas lights, ...e they the candles of yesteryear or their electric ...escendents, these decorations dazzle the beholder with the ...onder of Christmas.

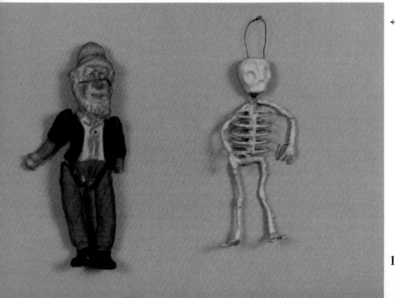

← Jointed composition man and skeleton ornament.

Wooden jumping jacks and a dancing couple who move as a top moves.

Two cotton dolls with paper scrap faces and crepe paper clothing beside a cotton Santa Claus.

Glass, cardboard, and tinsel rope was use
to make Santa Claus aircraft ornaments

Turn of the century fairy with a bisque
head and cloth body is 7 3/4" tall.

Wooden jester jumping jack is decorated
on both sides.

lass transportation ornaments.   Butterflies.

Glass Christmas trees.

Painted iron Christmas tree stand.

Painted tin Christmas tree stand.

Iron, tin and papier mache lighting fixtures for Christmas trees.

LIGHTING

Lights have always been one of the most inspiring aspects of Christmas. Traditionally, they were a symbol of Christ; a reminder that Christmas was a day to worship The Light of The World. They have since become an integral part of the Christmas ritual, not only for their religious meaning, but for their fiery beauty as well.

Before the birth of the electric light, candles were used to light Christmas trees. They were later replaced by electric lights in a rainbow of colors, and a variety of shapes. Today we can even buy lights that flash snycopically, and are guaranteed to last a lifetime.

It is exciting to see lights in every color of the spectrum winking from windows and sparkling on trees. But somehow they are not as picturesque as candles and old-fashioned lanterns.

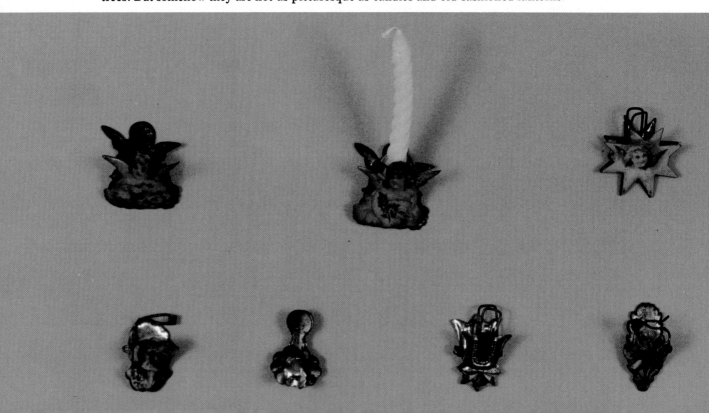

lass lanterns and painted tin clip-ons for Christmas tree candles.   Lanterns and paper candle shades.   ↑ ↓

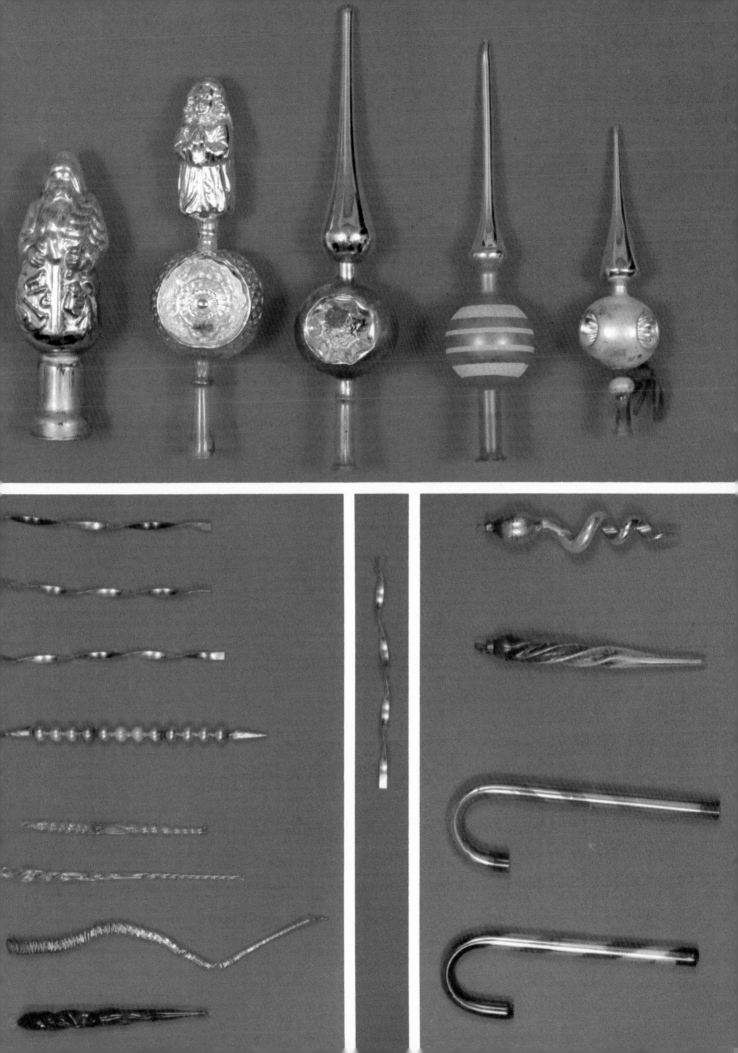

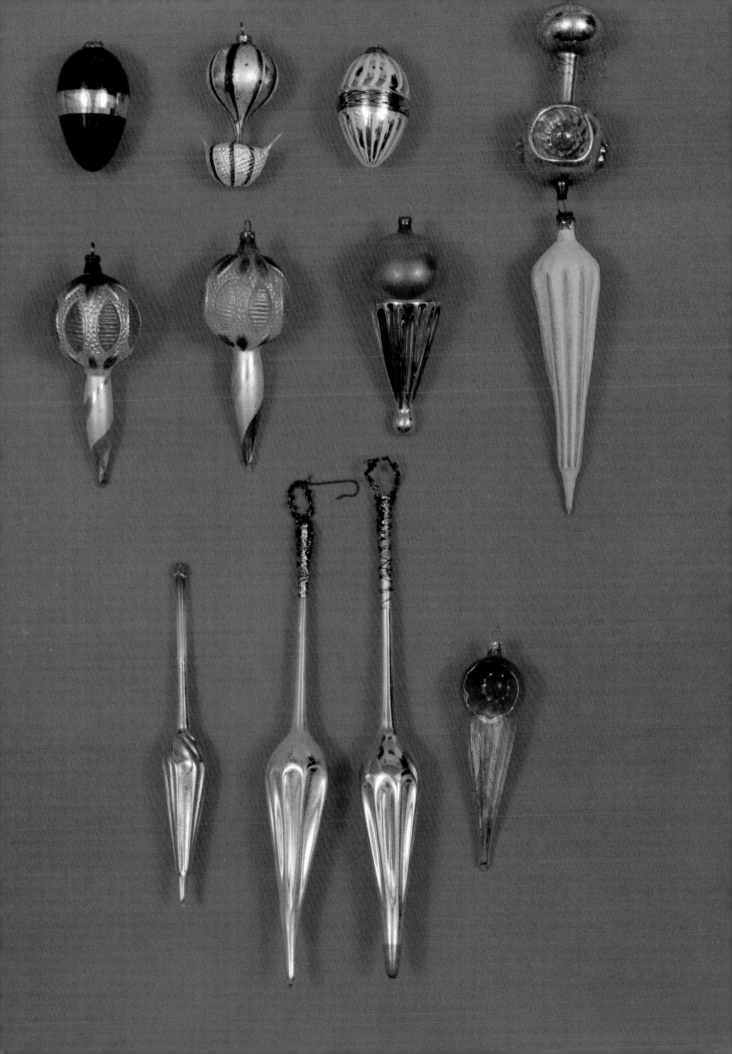

Christmas stockings:
Left—cotton child's stocking 15 1/2''
Right—Lithograph paper stocking 12 1/2''.

According to Christmas legends, the hanging of stockings began during the fourth century. The story goes as follows: A nobleman found himself in straitened circumstances after making some unwise investments. The unfortunate nobleman had three daughters who were nearly of an age to be married, but was unable to give them dowries. Although the young ladies were lovely and charming, without dowries they had little chance of finding husbands.

Bishop Nicholas of Myra, who was the inspiration for Santa Claus, heard of their circumstances and decided to correct the sorry situation. He went to the nobleman's home by night and tossed a purse of gold through an open window into one of the first daughter's

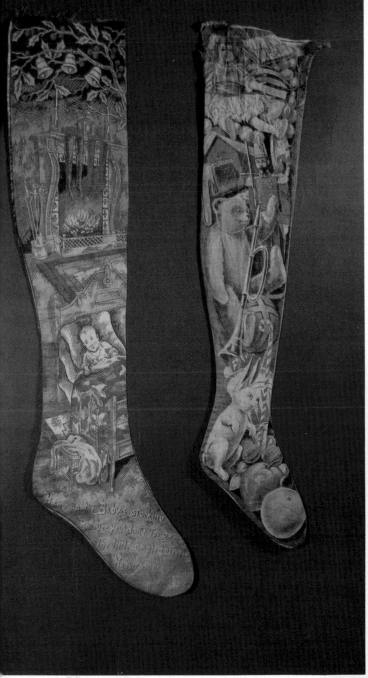

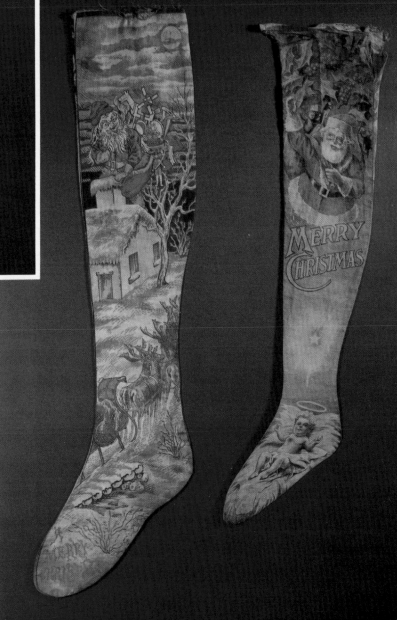

stockings, which had been hung by the fire to dry. Soon afterward, she married well. Nicholas repeated his benevolent errand when the second daughter grew old enough to be married.

By the time the third daughter came of age, the nobleman was overcome with curiosity. He kept a vigil to discover the identity of his kind patron, and caught him in the middle of his generous act. So grateful was the nobleman that he spread the tale far and wide. From then on, whenever an anonymous gift was received, it was believed to be a present from the good bishop. And even today, countless children hang their stockings by the fireplace in the belief that St. Nicholas will bring them their hearts' desires.

Cotton stockings (front and back views)
Left: 25''.
Right: 24''.

Printed paper Christmas tree made in Germany in 1890.

Oh how the tree quivered! What was to happen? The servants, as well as the young ladies, decorated it. On one branch there hung little nets cut out of colored paper, and each net was filled with sugarplums, among the other boughs gilded apples and walnuts were suspended, looking as though they had grown there, and little blue and white tapers were placed among the leaves. Dolls that looked for all the world like men — the tree had never beheld such before — were seen among the foliage, and at the very top a large star of gold tinsel was fixed. It was really splendid — beyond description splendid.

— *"The Little Fir Tree"*, Hans Christian Anderson

Sheep and goats made during
the early 20th century in Germany.

Metal reindeer made in Germany.

German "do good devil" candy boxes made of lithographed paper on wood during the 20th century.

Devil candy container made at the turn of the century in Germany is a Kemper figure. He is 9" tall, and has a papier mache face and hands, paper boots, and a cloth body. A crepe paper ruff encircles his neck, and he carries a candy basket on his back, with a silk tie addition.

Cotton snowman and animals from Germany.

Cotton and wood dogs made in Germany.

German Noah's Ark, mid 18th century.

ACKNOWLEDGMENTS

I would like to thank Tom Anderson, Noel Barrett, Bill Holland, Eleanor K. Ingersoll, Joan Kindler, Elizabeth Matlat, and Roy and Grace Olsen for all the sharing of their knowledge with me and continuous support throughout this project.

Unless otherwise noted, the photographs were taken by Judith Riddell and Fannie Stokes.
I wish to thank Judith Riddell, my editor, for the time she dedicated to working with me on the writing of this book.

PICTURE CREDITS

Collection of author except where acknowledged below.
Tom Anderson, 6, 7, 8, 23, 28, 36, 40, 53, 54, 55, 56, 57, 59, 97, 122
Bernard Barenholtz, photograph by Bill Holland, 2; about book, 3
Caroline E. Edelman, photograph by Robert Edelman, 36
Eleanor K. Ingersoll, 8, 24, 43, 122, 136, 139
Mr. and Mrs. Roy Olsen, 27, 37, 42, 77, 82, 90, 101, 131